# Contents

# Welcome to Pakistan

The Islamic Republic of Pakistan occupies the north-west corner of the Indian subcontinent. Pakistan came into being on 14 August 1947, when British rule in India ended. It was created as a homeland for India's Muslims. Its name comes from two Urdu words – *pak* (pure) and *stan* (land).

Pakistan originally consisted of two parts, one on each side of northern India. East and West Pakistan were separated by 1,600 kilometres. Then, in 1971, East Pakistan declared independence as Bangladesh, leaving West Pakistan as the country we know today as Pakistan.

Its people are as diverse as its terrain, with their own distinctive languages, dialects and customs. These have developed during a history lasting over 10,000 years.

DATABASE

## Neighbours

Pakistan sits in the middle of one of the world's most turbulent regions. It shares borders with Iran, Afghanistan, China and India. Wars and political instability across the region have slowed down the development of Pakistan's economy, industry, foreign trade and tourism.

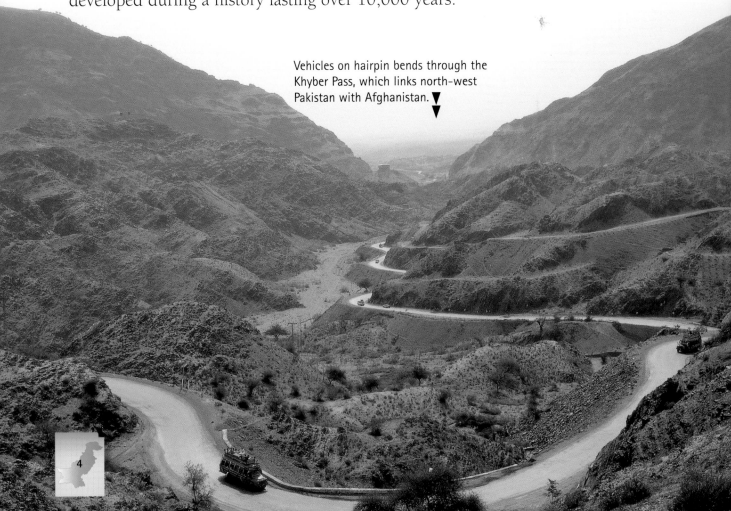

Vehicles on hairpin bends through the Khyber Pass, which links north-west Pakistan with Afghanistan. ▼

60°W    65°W    UZBEKISTAN    70°W    TAJIKISTAN    75°W

TURKMENISTAN

CHINA

KARAKORAM
RANGE

35°N

Khyber    HINDU    JAMMU and
Pass    KUSH    KASHMIR

Peshawar

AFGHANISTAN    ISLAMABAD
Rawalpindi

Kaitu

Kurram

Gumal    Sargodha

Gujranwala

Lahore

Faisalabad
Zhob    PUNJAB

Quetta    Multan    Sutlej    30°N

Sibi

PAKISTAN

Indus

KHARAN
BASIN    THAR
DESERT

Shikarpur    INDIA
Sukkur

BALUCHISTAN    Indus
HIGHLANDS    INDUS
Turbat    PLAIN

Dasht    Nal    Porali    Mirpur Khas

Gwadar    Hyderabad    25°N

SINDH

Karachi

IRAN

Tropic of
Cancer

ARABIAN    Mountains    △ Mountain peak

SEA    Grassland and farming

□ Capital    ○ Major city

Country boundary

N    0    300 Miles

W    E    0    300 Kilometres

S    20°N

# The Land

## Animals

**Mammals:**
Markhor (a goat, the national animal of Pakistan), Marcopolo sheep, Sindh wild goat, Himalayan ibex, musk deer, hog deer, black buck antelope, Eurasian brown bear, Asiatic black bear, common leopard, snow leopard, Asiatic cheetah, Eurasian lynx, grey wolf, golden jackal, striped hyena, Indian wild boar, red fox, Bengal fox, rhesus macaque, hanuman langur and porcupine.

**Birds:**
Partridge, warblers, shikra, blue rock pigeon, rock nuthatch, red-gilled chough, golden eagle, black eagle, Imperial eagle, black kite, Indian sparrowhawk, Saker falcon, kestrel, hobby, merlin, goshawk, Siberian crane, Eurasian crane, Indian peafowl, Egyptian vulture and bearded vulture.

**Reptiles and Amphibians:**
Monitor lizard, marsh crocodile, leopard gecko, Afghan tortoise, Indian python, Indian cobra, horned viper, green turtle, ant frog, tiger frog, cricket frog, burrowing frog and toads.

Pakistan is a land of extremes – from dry, dusty deserts in the south-east to fertile plains in the eastern and south-central regions and some of the highest mountains in the world.

Pakistan is divided in two by the Indus River, which starts in Tibet in China, flows across the Himalayas mountain range and into the north of the country. The Indus is joined by other rivers flowing from India, and it empties into the Arabian Sea in the south.

To the west of the Indus lie the Baluchistan Highlands. To the east lies the flat expanse of the Indus Plain. The Thar Desert straddles the eastern border with India. In the south, the coastal plain skirts the Arabian Sea. The Kharan Basin lies to the west of the Baluchistan Highlands. The Toba Kakar, Siahan, Kirthar and Sulaiman mountain ranges all pass through the Baluchistan Highlands.

The north-east of the country is crossed by the towering Karakoram mountain range, with the second highest mountain in the world after Everest – K2 (also known as Mount Godwin Austen) at 8,611 metres – and some of the biggest glaciers outside the polar regions.

Profile of the annual rainfall for Karachi on the coast of Pakistan. Total rainfall is less than one-third of London's. ▼▼

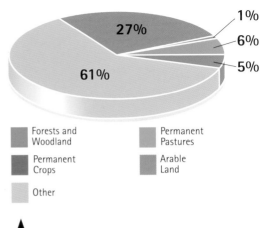

Land use in Pakistan. More than half the land is mountain and desert (defined as 'other').

- Forests and Woodland
- Permanent Crops
- Other
- Permanent Pastures
- Arable Land

## Growing mountains

Pakistan is so mountainous because the part of the Earth's crust on which it sits is pushing its way into the rest of Asia. In fact, the whole Indian subcontinent has travelled about 2,000 kilometres into Asia. The enormous forces between these colliding land masses has pushed the ground between them upwards, creating their vast mountain ranges. The process continues today, causing frequent earthquakes in the region.

## Climate

Pakistan has extreme variations in temperature and rainfall during the year and from place to place. There are three distinct seasons – the cool season (October – February), the hot season (March – June) and the wet season (June – October). During the wet season, the eastern and central plains receive abundant rain, but there is little rainfall in the arid southern and south-eastern desert regions.

Small villages and cultivation terraces cover the foothills of the Karakoram mountain range in northern Pakistan. ▼

### Plants

Pakistan's trees include: Spruce, evergreen oak, cheer pine, deodar (a type of cedar tree), alpine flora, pistachio, juniper, wild olive, wild ash, wild almond, fig, barbery, wild cherry and makhi.

# The People

Many of the peoples who settled in the Indian subcontinent over the centuries have handed down their distinctive cultures and customs through the generations to modern Pakistan. There is therefore no single, or typical, Pakistani culture.

Today, most of the people of Pakistan can be divided into five main ethnic groups – Punjabis, Sindhis, Pathans (Pashtuns), Balochs and Muhajirs. The Muhajirs are Muslim immigrants who moved to Pakistan from India after independence and their descendants. Punjabis are the most numerous group, followed by Sindhis.

Pakistanis, such as these fishermen in Karachi, are a mix of Indian, Chinese, east Asian and Arab peoples.

### Language

The official language of Pakistan is Urdu, but less than a tenth of the population speak it as their first language. About half of the population speak Punjabi, which is widely spoken in neighbouring northern India. English is also widely spoken in government, the military forces and higher education.

## Population and cultural changes

Pakistan's population has grown rapidly since the country's birth. By 1990, the population was more than three times its size in 1947. It continues to grow at the rate of about 2 per cent, adding nearly three million more people every year.

Pakistan society is patriarchal (male dominated). In most of the country, women have a lower status than men. Wealthier rural families and some urban families observe a practice called *purdah* in which women of all ages are hidden from view. They live screened off from visitors and they must cover themselves with concealing clothing when they go outside.

Purdah is in decline, however. The poorest families do not observe it because their women have to work. In the cities, too, fewer families observe it as more young women enter the workforce as independent, educated citizens.

▲ Children dress in similar traditional clothes to adults.

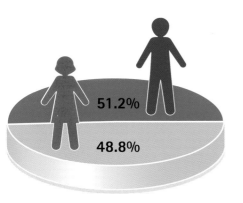

▲ There are more men than women in Pakistan's population.

51.2%

48.8%

DATABASE

### Ancient history

Stone Age people lived near modern Rawalpindi 50,000 years ago. By about 8500 BCE, people were farming crops in Baluchistan. Human settlements spread along the Indus River. By about 2600 BCE, they had developed into the Indus Valley civilization. This flourished until its sudden end in about 1750 BCE, perhaps because of a change in the climate.

 Web Search

► http://www.statpak. gov.pk
*General facts and figures from the Government of Pakistan Statistics Division.*

► http://www.cia.gov/cia/ publications/factbook/ geos/pk.html
*The Pakistan entry in the CIA World Factbook, with details of the country and its people.*

► http://unstats.un.org/ unsd/demographic/
*Population data provided by the United Nations Statistics Division.*

# Urban and Rural Life

The majority of Pakistan's population lives in the country's extensive rural areas. Living standards vary enormously between rural villages and major cities.

Pakistani families are especially close. It is common for two or three generations to live together. Wealthier urban families live in modern apartments or large houses. The less well-off may have only one or two rooms in which to house parents, children and grandparents, uncles and aunts. Homes and workplaces in cities are built from concrete or brick and have their own water supply and sewage system.

Most of Pakistan's cities have grown and developed naturally over centuries, but its capital city, Islamabad, is a modern planned city with streets laid out in a grid pattern. The city is divided into different zones for government, commerce, industry, residence and recreation.

33%  67%

■ Percentage of Population Living in Urban Areas

■ Percentage of Population Living in Rural Areas

▲
▲ Two-thirds of Pakistan's population live in rural areas.

A goatherd tends his flock on hills around his village in the Karakoram Mountains. ►►

## The Islamic Calendar

The passage of time in Pakistan's towns and villages is ruled by the Islamic calendar. Its starting point is the flight of the prophet Muhammad from Makkah (Mecca) to Medina, in Saudi Arabia, in CE 622. The Islamic calendar is lunar (based on the movements of the moon). A year has 354 or 355 days, and the 12 months are 29 or 30 days long.

## Village life

Living conditions in rural villages are more difficult than in the cities. Houses are often made from bricks held in place by mud or clay. The roof may be made from corrugated iron weighted down with rocks, or from branches and leaves. Rural houses often have no running water or sewage system, but there may be access to a shared clean-water supply such as a well or standpipe.

## Home produce

Most rural families produce at least some of their own food. It is common to keep a goat or two for milk and perhaps a buffalo to pull a plough. The milk is used to make cheese, butter and yoghurt. A variety of vegetables, beans and peas are grown. Meat may be in such short supply that it is eaten only on ceremonial occasions. Flour products, such as *naan* and *chapatis* (types of bread) are the dietary staples, washed down with *chai* (tea) or *lassi* (milk with the curds and butterfat removed).

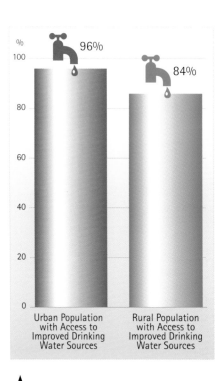

▲ Percentage of urban and rural populations with access to sources of clean drinking water.

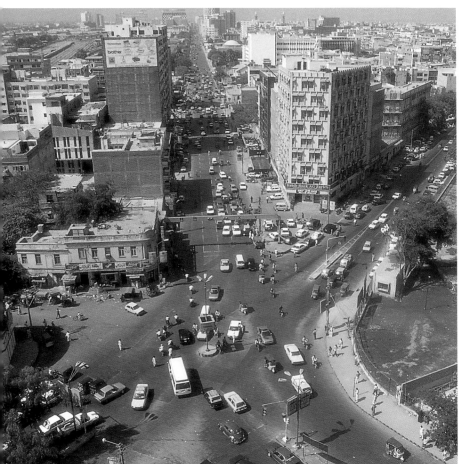

◄◄ A busy crossroads in Karachi. In the city centre there are apartment blocks and office buildings but no tall skyscrapers.

### Web Search ►►

► http://unstats.un.org/ unsd/demographic/ sconcerns/densurb/ default.htm
*Urban-rural population statistics for many countries including Pakistan.*

# Farming and Fishing

## Farming and fishing production

Major crops by weight:
Sugar cane  55,200,000 tonnes
Wheat       18,100,000 tonnes
Rice         4,650,000 tonnes
Cotton       1,768,000 tonnes

Fishing catch   616,500 tonnes

Agriculture is the most important part of Pakistan's economy. It employs about half of the country's workforce and contributes a quarter of its gross domestic product (GDP).

Wheat is the people's staple food and the most widely grown crop. Sugar cane, cotton and rice are grown mainly as cash crops. Cotton earns valuable export income and also supplies the domestic textile industry. Rice is grown mainly on the Indus River plain, where the soil is enriched by sediments washed down from the mountains.

One crop that has attracted worldwide attention is opium. A large proportion of the world's heroin – a harmful illegal drug – comes from opium poppies grown along the Pakistan–Afghanistan border. The government has been reducing this problem by giving farmers seed for other crops and providing alternative work for people.

**Farming Regions**

Pasture
Cropland
Forest
Mountain Region

Islamabad

Crops are grown mainly on fertile river plains. Goats are herded on the hills and mountain slopes.

Goats
Cereals
Rice

### Seasons and livestock

There are two main seasons for agriculture – *kharif* begins between April and June and ends between October and December; *rabi* begins in November or December and ends in April or May. The main winter crops are wheat, cumin and barley. In summer, onions, potatoes and several other vegetables are grown. Livestock farming produces milk, beef, mutton, poultry and wool.

## Irrigation

In Pakistan's driest areas, large numbers of water pumps have been installed to bring more water to the surface for agriculture. Pakistan now has one of the world's biggest irrigation systems, built with money from the World Bank and the US government, along the Indus and adjoining rivers. This has enabled the country to become self-sufficient in food grains. Unfortunately, each time the wet soil dries in the sun, a layer of salts forms on the surface, eventually making the soil infertile.

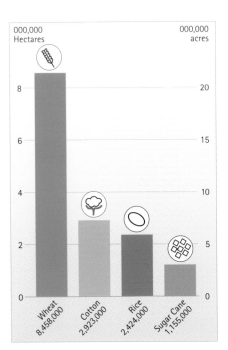

Area under cultivation in Pakistan for major crops. Wheat is by far the most widely grown crop.

A farmyard near Lahore. Most farmers still use animal power and simple machinery to cultivate the land. ▼

### Fishing

Most Pakistanis eat very little fish. The average consumption is only 2 kg per year – about one-third of the amount eaten in Britain or the US. The fishing catch includes sardines, anchovies and sharks. Shrimps, which make up a tenth of the catch, are highly prized because of their export value.

### Web Search ►►

► http://www.statpak.
  gov.pk/depts/aco/
  index.html
  *Details of Pakistan's crops from the government's Statistics Division.*

# Resources and Industry

:::: DATABASE ::::

## Mining and industrial production

Pakistan's mineral industry produces nearly 10 million tonnes of cement annually, mainly from the country's own limestone deposits.

| | |
|---|---|
| Cement | 9,500,000 tonnes |
| Coal | 3,116,000 tonnes |
| Pig iron | 1,500,000 tonnes |
| Crude steel | 500,000 tonnes |
| Gypsum | 377,000 tonnes |
| Soda ash | 230,000 tonnes |
| Caustic soda | 220,000 tonnes |
| Natural gas | |
| | 24 billion cubic metres |
| Crude petroleum | |
| | 20 million barrels |
| | (1 barrel = 42 gallons) |

Agriculture is so important to the Pakistan economy that the land itself is a valuable resource. Most of the country's natural resources are in the form of minerals extracted by mining or drilling.

In all, more than 20 different types of minerals have been found in commercial quantities. These include iron ore, salt, chromite, manganese, sulphur and copper. Iron ore is mined in large quantities, but it is mostly poor quality. Coal is mined, too, but most of it is also poor quality. Large reserves of limestone are mined to supply the cement-making industry. Oil, first discovered in 1915, contributes to Pakistan's energy needs. Extensive natural gas fields were discovered in the 1950s.

Pakistan's most important industry is cotton textile production. Other industrial products include steel, machinery, paper, chemicals, sugar, vegetable oil, food processing and fertilizer. Chemical production includes soda ash, caustic soda and sulphuric acid.

◄◄ Many wooden and metal products are still hand-crafted.

## Energy

Pakistan's energy needs are rising rapidly as more people use more electrical goods. Energy consumption has tripled since the 1980s. More than half of the country's electricity is generated by power stations that burn oil, gas or coal. Most of the rest is hydroelectricity, generated by water-powered turbines.

14

## Clothing and footwear

One of the fastest-growing manufacturing industries in Pakistan is the production of leather clothing, footwear and sports equipment. It is a very labour-intensive business employing more than 300,000 people. Other manufactured goods include pharmaceuticals, aircraft, machine tools, carpets, textiles and electrical goods such as light bulbs, televisions, radio sets and fridges.

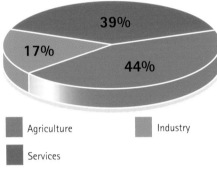

39%

17%

44%

Agriculture    Industry

Services

**Resources and Industry**

Industrial production is concentrated mainly along the coast and in the north-east.

Islamabad

Chemicals
Engineering
Iron and Steel
Textiles
Aerospace

Nearly half of Pakistan's workforce is employed in agriculture. 'Services' includes banking and insurance.

Teenage workers stitch together leather panels to make footballs for export.

## Web Search ►►

► http://www.mpnr.gov.pk
*Website of the Pakistan Mineral Development Corporation, established in 1974 to explore, plan, develop and operate mining ventures in Pakistan.*

► http://minerals.usgs.gov/ minerals/pubs/country/ 2002/afpkmyb02.pdf
*A downloadable report on Pakistan's mineral output from the US Geological Survey.*

► http://www.worldenergy. org/wec-geis/edc/ countries/Pakistan.asp
*Pakistan's energy production and use.*

# Transport

Pakistan is covered by an extensive network of roads, railways and air routes. Public transport within towns is mainly by buses, taxis, auto-rickshaws and *tongas* (horse-drawn carriages). Larger coaches, many of them air-conditioned, ply the highways between the major cities.

Pakistan's cities are connected by modern metalled highways. The GT (Grand Trunk) Road links Lahore and Peshawar. The Super Highway and National Highway run from Karachi to the interior of Sindh and Punjab. The Indus Highway runs between Peshawar and the southern Punjab. One of the most famous Asian roads, the Karakoram Highway, runs all the way from Islamabad to Kashgar in China. The RCD (Regional Co-operation for Development) Highway links Karachi with Quetta and on to Taftan on the Iran border.

### Railway network

Pakistan's national railway service carries 65 million passengers every year. It operates 228 mail, express and passenger trains daily. Since the 1990s, its diesel-electric locomotives have been built at a new factory near Peshawar, set up with help from Japan. It still runs much older steam trains in some places, especially for tourists.

◄◄ Coaches on a main road in northern Pakistan. Luggage is carried in roof racks.

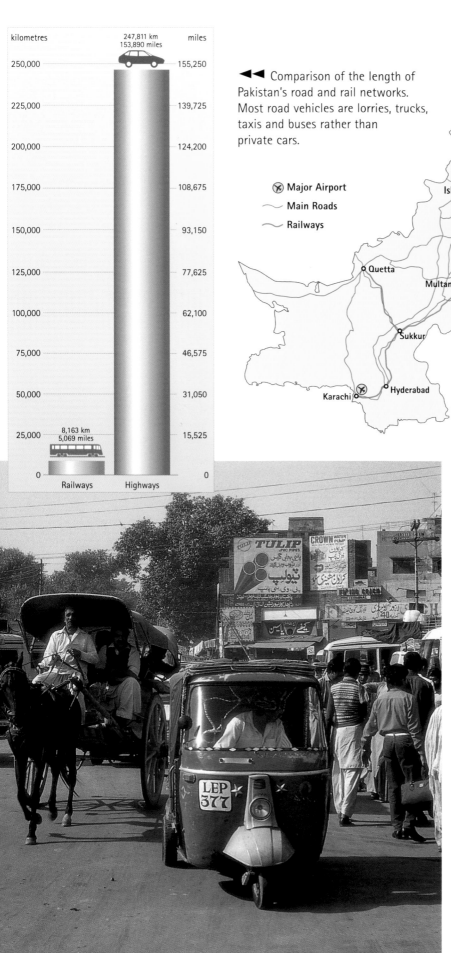

kilometres | 247,811 km / 153,890 miles | miles

250,000 — 155,250
225,000 — 139,725
200,000 — 124,200
175,000 — 108,675
150,000 — 93,150
125,000 — 77,625
100,000 — 62,100
75,000 — 46,575
50,000 — 31,050
25,000 — 15,525

8,163 km / 5,069 miles

0 — 0

Railways   Highways

◄◄ Comparison of the length of Pakistan's road and rail networks. Most road vehicles are lorries, trucks, taxis and buses rather than private cars.

## Transport

⊗ Major Airport
— Main Roads
— Railways

Peshawar
Islamabad
Rawalpindi
Gujranwala
Lahore
Faisalabad
Quetta
Multan
Sukkur
Hyderabad
Karachi

Most people travel between cities by road and rail – few Pakistanis can afford to travel by air. The major airports deal with both international and national flights. There are direct flights to Islamabad airport from most parts of Asia.

◄◄ In Lahore, people crowd on to small buses or hire motorized rickshaws or horse-drawn buggies to get around the city.

## 🌐 Web Search ►►

► http://pakrail.com
*Website of Pakistan's national railway service, Pakistan Railways.*

► http://www.piac.com.pk/
*Information on tourist destinations in Pakistan*

► http://www.pakboi.gov.pk/BFacts/roads.html
*Details of Pakistan's road network.*

# Education

Education in Pakistan is based on the system introduced during the period of British rule. The subjects taught are also similar to those taught in British schools – including maths, science and literature. In addition, there are classes in Urdu (the national language), English and Islamic studies.

Children enter primary school at the age of 5 and leave when they are 10 years old. They attend middle school for the next three years, until the age of 13. After that, secondary school lasts for another two years. Then, at the age of 15, they can go on to a technical secondary school or a higher secondary school for two years. For those who have the ability to go further, higher education is provided by universities and colleges.

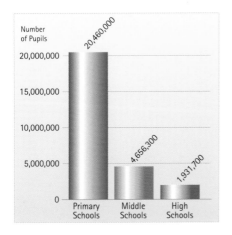

▲ Primary education is free, but many children are unable to attend school.

## Literacy and child workers

Despite having such a well-developed education system, the majority of the population is illiterate. The situation is worst in rural areas, where poverty prevents many children from attending school. Instead, they have to help to support their families by working in the fields, looking after the home or making things to sell.

Female literacy is particularly low. This is because less than one-fifth of girls finish primary school. To make matters worse, not all schools take girls. Only about one in four primary schools and one in three secondary schools accept girls. Some religious, political and other organizations are trying to help by setting up informal schools for girls in their own villages. The teachers are chosen from the local community and villagers have a say in what is taught. These informal schools can be set up in places where there are no state schools, because they cost less than 2 per cent of the cost of a state school.

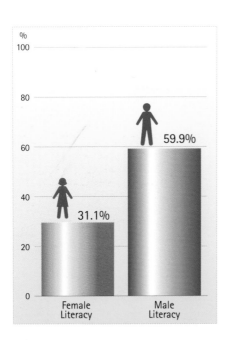

▲ Male literacy is low, but female literacy is even lower.

A schoolboy practises writing Urdu using chalk and a slate.

 An outdoor class at a school in north Pakistan.

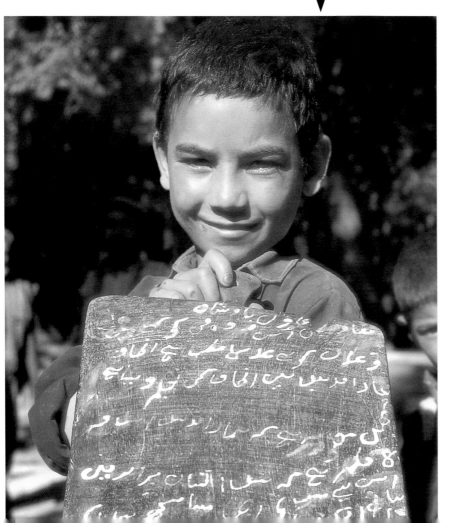

🌐 Web Search ▶▶

▶ http://www.statpak.gov.
pk/depts/fbs/statistics/
social_statistics/
social_statistics.html
*Facts and figures on social issues,
including education.*

▶ http://unstats.un.org/
unsd/demographic/
social/default.htm
*Literacy figures for many countries,
including Pakistan, from the United
Nations Statistical Division.*

▶ http://www.geocities.
com/Athens/Parthenon/
8107/univ.html
*Universities in Pakistan.*

# Sport and Leisure

Pakistan is a sporting nation. From the smallest village to the biggest cities, Pakistanis play games and follow the fortunes of their favourite teams with great enthusiasm.

Pakistan's national sport is hockey. The national team has won four world championships and gold medals at the Olympic Games. Pakistan also takes part in the Asian Games. In the 12 years they have been held the men's hockey team has won seven gold medals. Jahangir and Jansher Khan dominated squash in the 1980s and 1990s by winning 14 consecutive world championships. Pakistan's boxers, wrestlers and weightlifters have also won international honours.

## Tourism

Pakistan receives about 6 per cent of the total number of visitors who come to the whole of south Asia. Most come from the UK; more than half of these are visiting friends and relatives and another fifth are business travellers. About 15 per cent of visitors are holidaymakers and the remaining 2.5 per cent are religious tourists visiting Muslim sites and sacred places.

Polo started as a sport in Pakistan and neighbouring countries. ▼

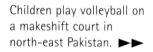

## Kabaddi

In addition to such team sports as cricket and hockey, a game called *kabaddi* is also popular. It is played by two teams who each try to capture players from the other team. It is thought the game developed in Pakistan about 4,000 years ago as a way of training people in hand-to-hand fighting.

Children play volleyball on a makeshift court in north-east Pakistan. ▶▶

## Cricket

Throughout the country, cricket is the most popular game. Successful players, such as Imran Khan and Waseem Akram, have become world-famous. A form of cricket called tape-ball cricket is very popular. Tennis balls are more readily available than cricket balls, but they are too light for cricket. To make them behave more like cricket balls, they have lots of sticky tape wrapped around them.

## Music

Until the 1980s, most of the music played and broadcast on TV and radio in Pakistan was traditional folk music. *Qawwali*, a form of music that comes from the Islamic religious tradition, is very popular. In recent years, Western rock music has grown in popularity, especially in the cities and among wealthier people. The most famous of Pakistan's music groups at home and abroad is Junoon. Their style is a blend of traditional and rock music.

 Web Search ▶▶

▶ http://www.sports.gov.pk
*The sports page of the Pakistan government website giving details of Pakistan's involvement in sports at national and international level.*

▶ http://www.cricinfo.com
*A cricket website with a section on the Pakistan team, its players and news of their matches.*

21

Muslim worshippers praying at a mosque.

## The Hajj

The Koran requires every Muslim to visit the holy city of Mecca, in Saudi Arabia, at least once. Mecca is the birthplace of the prophet Muhammad, the founder of Islam. During the annual pilgrimage to Mecca, called the Hajj, pilgrims perform a series of rites. Each year, many Pakistanis – often only adult males but sometimes whole families – make the journey to Mecca.

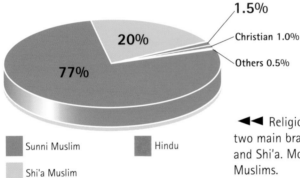

1.5%
Christian 1.0%
20%
Others 0.5%
77%

Sunni Muslim          Hindu
Shi'a Muslim

◄◄ Religion in Pakistan. There are two main branches of Islam: Sunni and Shi'a. Most Pakistanis are Sunni Muslims.

Most people shop for food in local street markets like this one in Quetta. ▼

# Daily Life and Religion

**D**aily life in Pakistan is dominated by the traditions of the Muslim faith and the teachings of its holy book, the Koran.

Daily life for a primary school child living on a rural farm begins at about 6.00 a.m. with washing and prayers. Then it is time for breakfast and a walk to school. After returning home in the afternoon, school homework and household chores have to be done. Only then is there time for playing with friends, before more prayers and then dinner. By 9.00 p.m. it is time for bed. At the weekend, when there is no school, work has to be done in the fields.

The diet in Pakistan consists of four main ingredients – *roti* (bread), *chaural* (rice), *sabzi* (vegetables) and *gosht* (meat). The meat may be anything except pork, because Muslims are not allowed to eat pork. Spices are often added to meals to flavour them.

## Marriage

Most marriages in Pakistan are arranged by parents. Marriage is seen more as a union between families rather than between individuals. A marriage is sometimes arranged before the couple have even met. It is traditional for the bride's family to present gifts of money or goods, called a dowry, to the groom's family.

## Religion

Pakistan is an Islamic state, but its constitution guarantees freedom of religion for its citizens. About 97 per cent of Pakistanis are Muslim. All Muslims are required to pray five times a day. Worshippers are called to prayer at a mosque – the Muslim place of worship – by an official called a *muezzin*. Women may attend prayers, but it is not a requirement for them.

Life expectancy in Pakistan is about 15 years less than in many Western countries.

### Dress

The national dress of Pakistan is the *shalwar-kameez*. The shalwar is a pair of loose-fitting ankle-length trousers gathered at the waist. The kameez is a long shirt-like top. On formal occasions, especially in the cities, women wear saris.

### Web Search ►►

► http://www.tourism.
gov.pk/events.asp
*Facts and figures about religion in Pakistan from the Government of Pakistan website.*

# Arts and Media

Cinema, broadcasting, music and magazines all play an important part in Pakistan society. The history of the region and the work of its artists are displayed in Pakistan's many museums and art galleries.

Cinema is the most popular form of entertainment. Small cinemas outside the major cities show mainly locally-made films. Urban cinemas show a mixture of Hollywood action movies and foreign films as well as traditional films. Lahore is the centre of Pakistan's movie industry, which is also known as Lollywood.

## Television and newspapers

Pakistan has its own, mainly state-run, television channels, but increasing numbers of people can now receive satellite television. Poorer rural families rely more on radio to receive news and entertainment. Magazines are very popular and offer wide-ranging coverage of current affairs, politics, sport, fashion and entertainment. Foreign newspapers and magazines are available in the cities.

**DATABASE**

## Museums and Galleries

Arts Council Gallery, Karachi
Baluchistan Archaeological Museum, Quetta
Moenjo Daro Museum, Moenjo Daro
Mughal and Sikh Galleries, Lahore Fort
National Museum of Pakistan, Karachi
National Art Gallery, Islamabad
Natural History Museum, Islamabad
Peshawar Museum, Peshawar
Quaid-e-Azam Museum, Karachi
Science Museum, Lahore

A cinema in Karachi.

## Museums and galleries

The National Museum of Pakistan, in Karachi, displays exhibits covering more than 7,000 years of history. Its galleries show pottery, metalwork, textiles and sculptures from different periods. In Karachi, the home of Quaid-e-Azam (Mohammed Ali Jinnah, the founder of Pakistan) has been preserved as a museum. His tomb is nearby and can be visited.

The museum at Moenjo Daro, in Sindh, is on the edge of one of the most important archaeological sites in south Asia. Moenjo Daro is thought to be the world's first planned city. It was built around 4000 BCE. Archaeologists have excavated it and visitors can now walk through it.

▲ An oil painting from the sixteenth century showing builders and their elephants constructing a building. The painting is on display in the Lahore Museum.

Numbers of TV and radio broadcast stations in Pakistan. ▼

TV Broadcast Stations
(total 22)

☐ =1 Station

Radio Broadcast Stations
(total 49)

📻 =1 Station

## 🌐 Web Search ▶▶

▶ http://www.heritage.gov.pk/
*Pakistan's museums and galleries, traditions and culture.*

▶ http://www.ptv-news.com.pk/
*Pakistan Television news.*

# Government

Pakistan has had a troubled and, at times, violent political past. Its democratically elected governments have been accused of corruption and dismissed by military leaders on several occasions. The latest military coup occurred in 1999, when General Pervez Musharraf seized power.

For administrative purposes, Pakistan is divided into four provinces, one territory and one capital territory. Each province is made up of between three and eight smaller areas called divisions. These are further divided into more than 100 districts. The disputed region of Kashmir in the north-east includes two districts that are controlled by Pakistan.

## The Provinces and their capital cities

| Province: | Capital: |
|---|---|
| Baluchistan | Quetta |
| North-West Frontier Province (NWFP) | Peshawar |
| Punjab | Lahore |
| Sindh | Karachi |

### Provinces and Territories

Pakistan's only local government territory is FATA – Federally Administered Tribal Areas – on the border with Afghanistan.

N.W.F.P.

F.A.T.A.

Islamabad

Punjab

Baluchistan

Sindh

Pakistan is administered from the capital, Islamabad, which is at the heart of Islamabad Capital Territory.

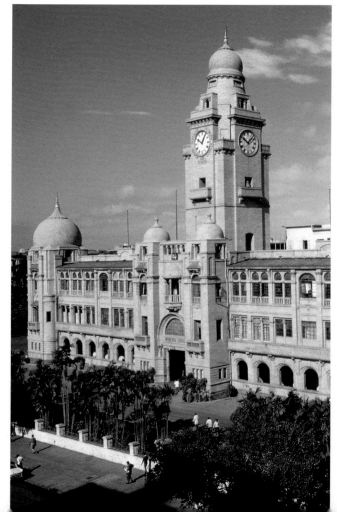

The City Hall in Karachi, the capital of Sindh province. ▶▶

## The president and Security Council

The president is the head of the government. Parliament is composed of two houses - the National Assembly and the Senate. The National Assembly has 217 seats. Of these, 207 seats are reserved for Muslim candidates and ten for non-Muslims, all elected by popular vote. Most of the 87 senators are selected by the provincial assemblies. The remainder, in the tribal areas, are elected by the people. National Assembly members serve for 5 years and senators for 6 years. One third of senators give up their seats every 2 years. The president is elected for 5 years by the National Assembly, the Senate and the four provincial assemblies. The prime minister is elected by the National Assembly.

Parliament was suspended in 1999 after a military coup. The new military president, General Pervez Musharraf, governed with the advice of a National Security Council of military chiefs and cabinet members. In 2002, the military leadership began to transfer power back to a newly elected parliament.

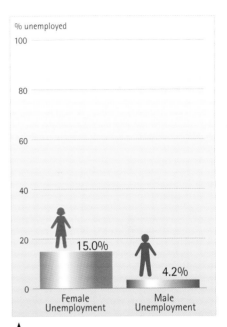

▲ Despite political upheavals, unemployment is not especially high but for religious reasons women often find it hard to get jobs.

◄◄ The royal palace at Hunza, Kashmir, an area in dispute with India over ownership and control. In the background are the Karakoram Mountains.

**Web Search** ►►

► http://www.pakboi.gov. pk/BFacts/provinces .html
*Pakistan's provinces and their boundaries.*

# Place in the World

People have lived in south Asia for thousands of years, but the modern Islamic Republic of Pakistan is a young country that is still developing its role in world affairs.

Pakistan is working to improve its economy by increasing exports, reforming its institutions, privatizing many of its industries and rooting out corruption. Pakistan's rapidly growing population places ever-growing demands on its limited resources. The situation has worsened with the arrival of large numbers of refugees from neighbouring Afghanistan. Many of these have fled from the war, led by US forces, to eliminate terrorists responsible for organising the attacks on the USA on 11 September, 2001.

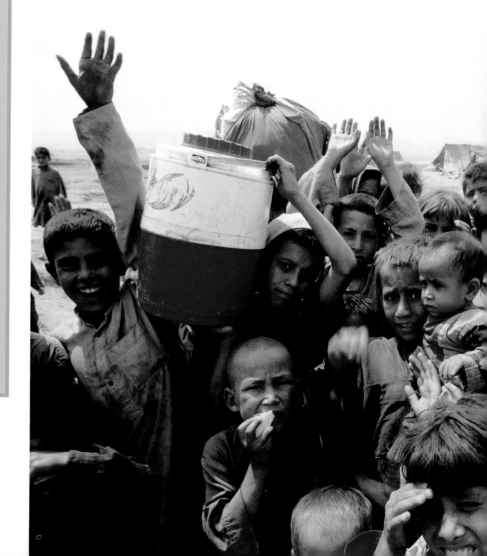

Afghan refugees in Jallozai, a refugee camp in Peshawar, Pakistan. ▶▶

28

Pakistan's ongoing dispute with India over the territory of Kashmir has sometimes erupted into violence. As both countries have nuclear weapons, military conflict between them is a matter of international concern. Pakistan's domestic political history has been troubled, too, alternating between civilian government and military rule.

## International links

Pakistan participates in many international organizations, including the United Nations (UN) and the World Health Organization (WHO). In addition, it is a member of a number of Asian organizations, including SAARC (the South Asian Association for Regional Co-operation). It is also a member of the Commonwealth, an association of countries that used to be British dependencies. Following the military coup in 1999 Pakistan's membership of the Commonwealth was temporarily suspended. It was restored in May 2004.

**EXPORTS**

£8 billion
(Cotton, sugar, rice, fruit, seafood, textiles, leather items, sports goods, carpets, handicrafts)

**IMPORTS**

£7.4 billion
(Industrial equipment, vehicles, iron ore, petroleum, edible oil, wheat, tea, fertilizer)

### Chronology of Historical Events from 1948

**1948**
War with India over Kashmir

**1958**
General Ayub Khan seizes power

**1959**
Rawalpindi is made the capital city

**1965**
New war with India over Kashmir

**1967**
Islamabad becomes the capital city

**1969**
General Yahya Khan seizes power

**1971**
East Pakistan becomes Bangladesh. Zulfikar Ali Bhutto is prime minister

**1977**
General Zia ul-Haq seizes power

**1979**
Zulfikar Ali Bhutto is hanged

**1988**
General Zia dies. Benazir Bhutto is elected prime minister

**1998**
Pakistani nuclear weapons tests

**1999**
General Pervez Musharraf seizes power

**2002**
After new elections, Mir Zafrullah Khan Jamali becomes prime minister under President Musharraf

**2004**
President Musharraf announces he will not resign as previously planned

◄◄ Pakistan's principal exports and imports and their comparative values.

**Area:**
803,950 sq km

**Population size:**
162,419,946

**Capital city:**
Islamabad (population 955,000)

**Other major cities:**
Karachi (12,200,000)
Lahore (6,400,000)
Faisalabad (2,500,000)
Rawalpindi (1,750,000)
Hyderabad (1,340,000)

**Longest rivers:**
Indus (2,896 km in Pakistan)
Sutlej (1,551 km)
Chenab (1,242 km)
Ravi (901 km)
Jhelum (825 km)
Beas (398 km)

**Highest mountain:**
K2, also known as Mount Godwin
Austen (8,611 m)

**Longest glaciers:**
Siachin (75 km)
Baltoro (62 km)
Batura (55 km)

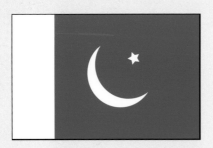

**Currency:**
Pakistani rupee
1 rupee = 100 paisa
£1 = approximately 112PRs

**Flag:**
Green with a vertical white band on the hoist side and a white crescent and star in the middle of the green part.

**Languages:**
Official language: Urdu.
English and Punjabi are widely spoken. Sindhi, Siraiki, Pashtu, Baluchi, Hindko, Brahui and Burushaski are also spoken.

**Major resources:**
Natural gas, oil, coal, iron ore, copper, salt, limestone

**Major exports:**
Textile products, rice, cotton, leather goods, sports shoes

**National holidays and major events:**
March 23: Pakistan Day
May 1: International Labour Day
August 14: Independence Day
September 6: Defence of
    Pakistan Day
September 11: Anniversary of the
    death of Quaid-e-Azam
    (Mohammed Ali Jinnah)
Religious holidays are based on the lunar calendar and so fall on different dates each year.

**Religions:**
Predominantly Muslim, also Hindu and Christian

# Glossary

**AGRICULTURE**
Farming the land, including ploughing, planting, raising crops, and raising animals.

**ALTITUDE**
The height above sea level of a mountain or an area of land.

**CASH CROP**
A crop grown for sale, especially to another country.

**CLIMATE**
The long-term weather in an area.

**CULTURE**
The beliefs, ideas, knowledge and customs of a group of people, or the group of people themselves.

**ECONOMY**
A country's finances.

**EMPIRE**
A group of colonies – countries in other parts of the world – ruled by one country.

**EXPORTS**
Products, resources or goods sold to other countries.

**FERTILE**
Soil rich in nutrients that make it ideal for growing crops.

**GOVERNMENT**
A group of people who manage a country, deciding on laws, raising taxes and organizing health, education and other national systems and services.

**GROSS DOMESTIC PRODUCT**
The value of all goods and services produced by a nation in a year.

**IMPORTS**
Products, resources or goods brought into the country.

**ISLAM**
The religious faith of the world's Muslims. Islam was founded by the prophet Muhammad.

**LITERACY**
The ability to read and write.

**LITERACY RATE**
The percentage of the population who can read and write.

**MANUFACTURING**
Making large numbers of the same things by hand or, more commonly, by machine.

**MONSOON**
A seasonal wind that blows across south Asia from the south-west in summer, bringing heavy rain.

**POPULATION**
All the people who live in a city, country, region or other area.

**PROVINCE**
A part of a country that has a particular identity, often with its own local government.

**REPUBLIC**
An independent country whose head of state is an elected president, not a king or queen.

**RESOURCES**
Materials that can be used to make goods or electricity, or to generate income for a country or region.

**RURAL**
Having the qualities of the countryside, with a low population density.

**SUBCONTINENT**
A large distinctive land mass that is part of a continent. The Indian land mass, which includes Pakistan, is a subcontinent of Asia.

**URBAN**
Having the qualities of a city, with a high population density.

# Index